T0196057

IT'S MY ABSOLUTE
Pleasure

A GUIDE TO EXCELLENT SERVICE,
A PROMISE FOR A BETTER YOU

IMANI N. ROBINSON

WESTBOW
PRESS®
A DIVISION OF THOMAS NELSON
& ZONDERVAN

WestBow Press books may be ordered through booksellers or by contacting:

WestBow Press
A Division of Thomas Nelson & Zondervan
1663 Liberty Drive
Bloomington, IN 47403
www.westbowpress.com
1 (866) 928-1240

ISBN: 978-1-9736-9015-3 (sc)
ISBN: 978-1-9736-9016-0 (e)

Print information available on the last page.

WestBow Press rev. date: 04/14/2020

Contents

I give special thanks to God the Father, Son, and Holy Spirit who keeps me, helps me, protects & directs me. You are my Everything and I Love You!

To my husband, Sredrick Robinson, my children, my mom & dad, family & friends, thank you for your love & support. Thanks to every youth I've served

To my mentors Diane K, Lois E, Nancy E, and the Author Learning Center.

My prayer partner, Mrs. Lillie Booker.

To the Walkers for the season of training ground allocated for me to be used by God, to serve the church and God's people. With everything, He gave me to give, I gave. I love you all.

To my accountability partners, friends and sisters: Alisha, Angela, Candace, Darcella, Mary Ann and Stacie G, thank you.

I release this book with prayers for DeVos Urban Leadership Initiative. Thank you for empowering me to expand the capacity in which I will continue to grow and empower other servant leaders. Thank you for encouraging me to continue to live "outside the box".

INTRO…
To Serve is a Gift, A gift from God.

God gave me the gift of serving. Why? So, I can be taken advantage of? So, I can get a lot of praises? So, I can out serve the next person? No… no… no… Those are all code violations.

My servants' heart is so that God will be glorified, that people will see Him in my service

If I am lifted, I will draw man to Myself.

Everything good that is done is ONLY because God lives in me to do His perfect will.

EVERY good gift comes from God.

It is important to know God is our Mover, our Promoter and Prompter of all good.

Once He brings you to that understanding of who He is, NOTHING CAN STOP YOUR SERVICE TO HIM IN HIM.

God is Love. To know Him is to love Him. To Love Him is to serve Him. Love & serve all people.

I am so glad you are here because if you are continuing to read, you have a servant's heart, or you desire to have a servant's heart. You are the community I am looking for. Thank you for being one of the best people in our country!

Why? Because you have a desire to serve. And to serve well.

Side bar: Now, I do know there are some who read books just to criticize. You are welcome here as well. We will view your criticism as feedback and trust that God will use it for our good for continued growth… God bless you.

As I stated before, this book is especially for those who desire to serve and serve well. In each chapter following, you will go on a journey with guidance on how to serve well.

As a wife, minister, mother, entrepreneur and philanthropist, I will share prayers and instructions from my personal experiences with God and people that I know will improve your churches, organization, and or businesses. It will help you enhance your service to others and start your "My Absolute Pleasure" builder.

What is" My Absolute Pleasure Builder?" It is a perspective. A mindset and heart set that says in EVERYTHING you do, it is your "Absolute Pleasure" to do so. For Real.

A Lifestyle of Repentance

The first step of having a heart of service and to live for God, is having a lifestyle of repentance. Daily confession of imperfection, acknowledging sin in our hearts.

Real pure honesty... Pray, Cleanse me of ALL UNRIGHTEOUSNESS. Father forgive me.

Journal what your struggles are and a personal journal to God letting Him know you trust Him.

Motives

According to God's word, we should be servants. (Eph.4:12) Pray: I desire to have your character. Help my motives to be pure out of obedience to You. Help me to see the needs of others as being more important than my own. Help me not to look for praises or gifts in return. I just want to serve as unto You because, it is Your will. In Jesus name, Amen. Ask God to give you a desire to serve Him and others in Humility and Love.

Now, ask someone who you know loves you, do they see you as a servant of God. Why or why not?

Write what they said, and then journal how you feel about their answer. How can you get better in serving? Journal...

Faith

Believing God will do what He says Ask to increase your faith in knowing He will give you His heart to serve. Pray & ask and it will be. Why? Because that is God's will.

Do you believe God will do what He says He will do? Think about a time when you believed God for something, and it came to pass. Journal about it...

You Have Not Because You Didn't Ask...

Sincerely ask God to help you. And I guarantee He will.

Journal about some areas in your life where you have been selfish, and want God to take that and use it for His glory to be a blessing to someone else...

Works

Faith without works is dead. Volunteer Ask God to show you where He wants you to serve and who you should be serving.

Journal about those places. Why would God want you to serve there?

Leave You at the Door

Rely on God. You will be amazed in the ways God will use you, when you surrender your will to His.

Pray, Lord I give my will and my life to you, to do with it what You want to do. Send me Lord, I will go.

Journal what God is saying to you and then ask Him to confirm your assignment...

Obey

Do what God tells you to do. God has a specific plan for your life. When you get your assignment for Him. Do it with everything in you, Do it unto Him. Do it with love. Do it with excellence.

PRAY for the Shaders and the Spirit Crushers

With service, comes spiritual war as well.

You will be angry when the shaders and the spirit crushers come. What are shaders and who are they? Shaders is a terminology used formerly as "Player haters", "Haters", Jealous folks". Let me give you some identifiers, they will say things to you like:

- **"You are doing too much"**
- **"You are always so busy"**
- **"Girl/Man, you are all over the place"**

They will use different ways or words in the effort to distract or discourage you from doing good. In bible days, they were called the naysayers. You may get angry at first but remember to keep the right perspective... we don't wrestle with flesh and blood. God promises if we keep our minds focused on Him, we will have PERFECT PEACE. Stay focused, pray for them and trust Gods leading. Remember, Who you asked for a heart of service, has given you a heart of service. Some will not understand. And it's ok. Keep doing the will of God.

Search me oh God

Commit to asking God daily to rid you of ANYTHING that is not like Him. Tell Him. I want Love, kindness, meekness, patience, joy, goodness, faithfulness, and self-control.

Journal about each of the fruit above..

CHAPTER 10

A Special Chapter to Nonprofit and/ or Religious Organizations (Especially the church)

Perspective is everything... Listen to it. It will tell you who you are and what you need to work on... 1st Example: When you see ANYONE doing something that is good and beneficial to others, and your first thought is; that's great. I wonder if

- I could help in some way.
- Or I'd like to "find out" how could I start something like that in my community?
- Or, what I believe is the best response; Ask God, could you use me like that? I would then say, you have the potential of being one of the most loving, selfless, impactful, and successful human beings in the world. Why? You have the " My Absolute Pleasure" builder.

Another Perspective when you see ANYONE doing something good to benefit others and your response is the following:

- They are showing off.
- They are doing too much.
- They just want to be seen. I would say that is a serious heart condition and you need to immediately ask God for a heart transformation.

You see, when your perspective is negative, your response to good will be negative. The cause for this response could be a number of things: jealousy, insecurity, confused identity. It could be envy. hate, pain, or a lack of confidence. This is dangerous for you, your community and those you may influence. How do you change?

First, you must know you need to change. You must desire to change, and you must ask the Creator to search your heart and transform it. I promise you this will, His will, will work.

Write a letter to God, asking Him to clean you up. Repair you. Restore you. To help you. So that you will be a help and not a hurt to the Body of Christ..

Hurt people, do what? Hurt people.

When it Seems you Failed, Don't Give Up. Go Back to Chapter One and Repeat

Journal one paragraph why you think you failed...

_____

_____

_____

_____

_____

_____

_____

_____

_____

_____

_____

_____

_____

_____

_____

_____

_____

_____

SCRIPTURE REFERENCES:

1 John 3:18

1 John 4:7-21

John 14:1-10

1 Peter 2:1-10

Ephesians 4:1-10

John 13:12-14

Galatians 5:13-14

1 Peter 4:10-11

Philippians 4:13

Mark 10:44-45

Mark 9:35

Matthew 10:28

Ephesians 4:12

Galatians 5:13

Final Application- Now to Him who can do exceedingly abundantly (immeasurably) more than all we ask or imagine, according to His power that is at work within us.

Ephesians 3:20

Support Love In Action Ministries at www.loveinactionstl.org

Printed in the United States
By Bookmasters